MW01675266

PERFECT CO

How to Improve your Communication Skills

Jeffrey Trotter

CONTENTS

INTRODUCTION ...4

CHAPTER 1: COMMUNICATION SKILLS - A VEHICLE ON THE ROAD TO SUCCESS ...9

CHAPTER 2: THE ART OF LISTENING ...23

CHAPTER 3: PUBLIC SPEAKING SKILLS: PUBLIC SPEAKING FEAR COMES FROM PERCEIVED FAILURE ...35

CHAPTER 4: COMMUNICATION SHOULD BE NATURAL – SO WHY DO WE FIND IT CHALLENGING? ...50

CONCLUSION ...100

INTRODUCTION

"Your ability to communicate is an important tool in your pursuit of your goals, whether it is with your family, your co-workers or your clients and customers." - Les Brown.

It derives from the Latin word "communicare," which means to share. Communication is the process of sending and receiving signals or messages between two parties. It can be done in a variety of ways, including verbally (using words), in writing (using printed or digital media like books, magazines, websites, or e-mails), visually (using maps, charts, or graphics), or even nonverbally (using body language, gestures, tones, and voice pitch). Communication skills encompass a wide range of other elements, such as our body language, gesticulation, facial expression, posture, listening skills, pitch, and tone of voice, in addition to how we interact with others.

Today's highly competitive world requires effective communication skills, whether oral or written. According to Robert Anderson, communication is the exchange of ideas, opinions, or information through speech, writing, or visuals. Written communication refers to communication using written symbols (either printed or handwritten).

It is a method that we employ to establish and modify relationships in all spheres of life, not just the commercial world. It promotes healthy relationship development and helps to avoid insults, arguments, and conflicts. Effective communication skills are now a crucial consideration when hiring and choosing any potential candidates. Many interviewers evaluate candidates during the interview process based on their communication skills.

Many professionals agree that effective communication abilities can increase an individual's productivity, effectiveness, and interpersonal relationships both inside the department and with the rest of the company as well as with the general public. Even if you look at any job advertisement, the most of them state that candidates should have strong communication skills.

Since technical qualifications are likely to be more or less the same for every applicant, having good communication skills helps you stand out from the competition during interviews. Promotions are frequently assumed to go to those who can communicate effectively regardless of the type of job, position, or department, i.e. from senior level to lowest management level. In actuality, as one's career progresses, the need of effective communication skills increases; every manager and leader must be able to speak, listen, ask thoughtful questions, and write clearly and concisely. A skilled communicator recognises their communicational skills and weaknesses that stand in the way of effectively conveying their message. They identify the cause of the situation and look for workable solutions.

Good communication skills are beneficial to anyone in all facets of their life, not just their professional one. In the present business environment, the ability to communicate information accurately and effectively is not only acceptable but also required in every organisation, thus it shouldn't be overlooked.

The most critical factors that must be taken into account by each and every individual for effective communication include the ability to speak appropriately with a wide variety of people, maintaining eye contact, using vocabulary appropriately, customising our language to suit the audience, active listening, presenting our ideas appropriately, writing concisely, and being a team player.

Why Should Everyone Choose Training in Communication Skills?

Good communication also involves people being able to write and construct emails.

A few benefits of attending a communication training are as follows:

You'll be happier.

Your happiness increases when you have the appropriate communication skills. A very common misconception that you may have heard is that happiness cannot be purchased with money. The right acts can be taken to achieve happiness. With the great communication at your disposal, you may take the actions that make you happy. Correct communication abilities make it simpler for you to perform the action that makes you pleased.

This could involve landing the job you've always desired or meeting potential clients and pitching your ideas to them. All of this depends on your ability to communicate well.

When you choose a communication skills training programme, you evaluate it and understand how to use it to your advantage. Good communication makes it simpler for you to avoid verbal altercations, better manage your rage, and change your relationships with the people around you so that you can communicate with them easily.

It makes you appear more attractive.

With the proper communication, you can draw new individuals into your life. That is sufficient justification to attend a communication skills training. With effective communication skills, you may attract and bring like-minded others into your life. This has nothing to do with any mystical jargon. The logic is rather basic. You must strive to become a fun-loving, kind, and optimistic person if you want to attract others who are fun-loving, confident, and kind into your life. With communication skills training, you may improve how you speak and express yourself. It enables you to benefit from good communication. It enables you to boost your self-esteem, confidence, and social life. each of which are regarded as attractive qualities.

Good communication is essential for success.

The single most important factor that will contribute to your success is interpersonal skills. Whatever field or industry you are in, having the correct communication skills will greatly increase your chances of meeting the right people and exploring new opportunities. These "skills" will help you improve and give you the upper hand over your rivals. One of the many wonderful benefits of having good communication is success.

Just a brief list of the benefits of good communication is provided here. Nobody is born with the ability to communicate well; people learn it over time. By choosing a training programme, you can dramatically improve your communication skills.

CHAPTER ONE

Communication Skills - A Vehicle On The Road to Success

Babies begin learning how to communicate from the moment of birth, building on their natural ability to communicate with their mothers through crying. After then, throughout life, a person's growth and advancement depend on communication in one form or another, whether they are speaking with others or receiving communication from them. Communication skills are a very valuable advantage for anyone looking to succeed.

All organisms in nature depend on being able to communicate, and humans are no different in that regard. Of course, we view human communication as significantly more complex and specialised than that of other species. We employ a variety of venues and communication methods as a species. However, for the purposes of this book, we shall concentrate on interpersonal communication skills because they may be essential for success in many fields of endeavour.

It goes without saying that the majority of big businesses and organisations include communication skills in their training programmes for their staff members' career growth. Most businesses and non-profit organisations will benefit greatly from the long-term profitability and efficiency of their employees who have strong communication skills. For those who require certain communication skills, such public speaking, special training programmes may be scheduled internationally, contracted outside, or the employee sent on an external course.

Few people in business would disagree that the greater your communication abilities, the more success you are likely to have, and the more likely it is that your career will advance in the future. Although there are undoubtedly other factors that contribute more to success than communication abilities, their potential contribution is undeniable.

The Benefits of Good Communication Skills

The benefits of good communication skills are too numerous and varied to list here; they may one day save your life, win the heart of your ideal partner, or even prevent your marriage from falling apart.

However, some of the main advantages of improving your communication skills in business are as follows:

1. Managing Your Staff Effective, two-way communication is a key component of staff management. Your capacity to manage will be limited and may even be harmful to the morale of your staff if you are incapable of communicating with those who are under your control. Effective communication is important for delegation, employee motivation, understanding, and training, among other things.

Good communication with your staff can help you with their motivation, either directly or by encouraging their own motivation, or both. Simply put, effective communication skills will help you become a better manager.

2. Interacting with people Outside the Organization Whether you work for a business, the government, or another form of organisation, your job may require you to interact with people outside the organisation in person or over the phone. In these situations, effective communication skills have a dual function because you are both the organization's and your own representative, making your performance doubly crucial. firstly to the

organization's or company's reputation, and secondly to your professional success.

3. Developing Self-Belief

Your self-confidence will rise as your communication abilities do, therefore enhancing any communication skills may be a crucial component of your long-term success strategy.

There are numerous more advantages to developing your interpersonal communication skills in many facets of your life.

Ways to Improve Communication Skills

Communication skills training programmes are commonplace, and if you're lucky, your employer, if you're not already employed, will have a course or set of courses they can arrange for you. The type of course you should take depends on the reason you need it; for example, a course on public speaking would differ from one on communicating with your staff or employees. Additionally, you can get courses in oral communication skills, telephone skills, and written communication skills. It truly comes down to deciding, together with your boss, if you have one, which course is the top priority for you.

Speaking to staff or to groups of people at every opportunity might be important because practise is also essential. Three more points should be kept in mind: 1.

Communication is two-way. It's not only a matter of you speaking to your employees. You must encourage kids to openly communicate with you as well. That might not always be simple, therefore interpersonal skills really come into play in this situation. Being a good listener is a crucial talent; in fact, I think being a good listener is a very powerful personal quality to possess.

2. Always keep in mind that the person you are speaking to is an individual; a group is made up of individuals. Over the years, I've managed more than 100 employees in a variety of settings, including my own business in England in the 1990s. Knowing and understanding each of those individuals was always crucial because they were all wholly unique.

3. Improving your memory might be especially important if you have a lot of staff or employees reporting to you because an excellent manager needs to be able to understand each person as an individual. Remembering them as an individual anytime you need to speak with them can be comforting for them and advantageous for the two of you.

Memory can be a significant factor in other forms of communication. Speaking to a group of people from memory is a tremendous boost to your confidence and effectiveness while giving a public speech, for instance. A public speaker's ability to make an impact is significantly diminished if they must constantly refer to notes.

Additionally, memory can be a valuable advantage when presenting ideas, work, and proposals to your supervisors. If you are aware of all the pertinent details, it will not only help your case but will also give the appearance that you are sharp and on top of your game.

Although communication is a difficult subject, you must start somewhere if you want to develop your communication skills. Perhaps the best place to start is with your weaknesses, therefore it might be helpful to talk to your boss about that. If you don't have a boyfriend, personal friends whose opinions you respect and trust could be another source of advice.

Knowing How To Improve Communication Skills

It's not the simplest of chores to develop effective communication abilities, particularly if you don't know how to approach self-improvement in general. The development of excellent communication skills and the enhancement of existing interpersonal abilities are immensely positive steps for anyone. Developing one's communication skills, both at work and at home, will have good effects, including an increase in happiness and productivity. Stronger communication fosters an increase in trust and understanding, both of which help you form more lasting and enduring connections with those around you.

Being creatures of habit, human beings have a difficult time changing their communication skills. This is why many people struggle with this. Our capacity for communication grows throughout childhood and into adulthood. They are deeply ingrained inside us; they do not develop or adjust quickly. Changes, even good ones, require us to step outside of our comfort zone and let go of our defences against the opinions of others. We must lay down our weapons and plunge headfirst into the turbulent sea of life. It is a complicated issue. People are frequently hesitant to part with the tools and supports that have prevented them from being perceived as what they fear others would see. Sometimes people are reluctant to acknowledge that they require assistance or that their skills need to be improved, claiming that the first step to solving a problem is acknowledging that you have one.

The best place to start when learning how to effectively communicate is with a thorough evaluation, first of the skills demonstrated and then of the areas that require work and the best way to approach those improvements. It is best to complete this process alongside another individual. As communication skills develop early in life, people may develop "blind spots" in their habits—areas or skills in which they fall short without realising it. Other times, people acquire certain abilities at a younger age and their personalities develop around those communication skills to the point when using other talents feels like pretending to be someone they are not. However, it's crucial to avoid being defensive about the procedure. No one is attempting to alter who you are; rather, they are attempting to provide you with additional tools to express who you are. Your communication abilities can increase your likeability, diversity, and emotional intelligence. Stronger person. Be wary of any cookie-cutter approaches to improving or evaluating your communication skills; individuals might differ greatly from one another, and improvement methods should take this into account.

Although the final results should be comparable for all, as a well-rounded set of communication skills should appear to be the same for everyone, the significant differences come in the form of the less-traveled path. People learn in a variety of ways and at varying rates, and some people will have more to learn than others. Some people will need to practise their skills more to make sure they are fully integrated into their repertoire of effective communication skills. Additionally, each person will have distinct schedules and time frames into which this self-improvement must be fitted.

The process of developing communication skills is one of self-improvement and, as such, has inherent positive effects on one's personality, mood, and quality of life. Even the most basic "how to improve communication skills" templates will have positive results.

The process for you could be as easy as: self-evaluating the skills you don't know you have but use in everyday human interaction; identifying issues or contradictions in your range of actions, words, tones, or grammar; finding situations where you feel comfortable enough to make changes (like with your close friends or family); and putting these new or unused skills to use. If you feel comfortable enough to do so, it can be beneficial to ask for feedback. If not, make sure to carefully monitor your progress during the improvement process.

As always, patience is crucial. Take your time; it can be a while before you reach your desired level of successful communication. Anything worth doing is worth doing well, and any type of self-improvement should never be rushed. As with other things, developing strong communication skills requires practise, and plenty of it. For this reason, the student must not be hesitant to practise what they have been working on in the public sphere. One of the barriers to the process of improving oneself and a common roadblock is the need to "put oneself out there."

Communication Skills: How To Improve

For many people, it is challenging to comprehend how to increase communication skills, and in the majority of cases, it is simple to understand why. Many people find interacting with others uncomfortable and frequently worry about outside their comfort zone in terms of communication. In other instances, people are unaware that they may stand to enhance their communication skills. Therefore, the improvement process necessitates assessing an individual's current skills, determining where a change would be beneficial, and, more crucially, determining the best method for implementing that improvement.

Any strategy for correction should start with an awareness of what communication skills are. They include the tactile components of communication, such as speaking, writing, reading, and listening, but they also include more specialised abilities, such empathetic and active listening, appropriate bodily reaction and response, and context comprehension. We gain communication skills over time through many hours of interaction with other people. Unfortunately, during this development, we pick up bad habits that are frequently difficult to break.

Understanding how to enhance communication skills is advantageous since, in certain cases, people's communication abilities suffer from a halted development throughout their formative years and they enter adulthood lacking effective interpersonal communication skills. People frequently claim that their personality determines their communication style and, consequently, their interaction skill set, however it is possible to argue that our communication development influences our personality in a variety of ways. Our communication style and abilities shape our public image and sense of self. Developing your communication skills will change how those around you see you and strengthen your relationships with them.

While a how-to template will help you improve your communication skills, it's crucial to remember that any template must be tailored and customised to the needs of the individual. The ultimate objectives and targets will remain rigid and fixed in amount, but there is always room to modify your own how-to plan from the template's fundamental structure. For example, some self-improvement programmes need a specific volume and style of practise that might not be compatible with your time restrictions or comfort level.

Self-improvement is a crucial stage in the process of human development, and there are many benefits to actively seeking to improve one's flaws. Before deciding how to improve communication abilities, it is crucial to think about why you want to invite change. Effective interpersonal communication is a crucial component of a healthy lifestyle, and any effort to improve it is a worthwhile endeavour. How many hours a day do you spend communicating and interacting with those around you, for the moment? When you woke up this morning, was it with a loved one? on the way to work, with the bus driver? The salesperson in the morning coffee shop? Your seatmate as you discuss your most recent assignment in the classroom? As soon as your immediate boss gives you a report on that order.

How to Improve Communication Skills Template

1. Observe how you interact with individuals around you with care and consideration. Examine your speaking style, paying attention to your tone, volume, and accent. Examine your writing style, paying particular attention to spelling, punctuation, tone, and vocabulary.

2. Identify any issues, conflicts, or contradictions in the way you interact with the people around you. These problematic areas will serve as the focal point of your improvement strategy.

3. Determine the circumstances in which you feel comfortable and uncomfortable implementing change.

4. Adjust your current goals to integrate newly discovered short-term targets.

5. Find opportunities to "practise" and look for venues for feedback along the process. Self-monitoring and review are also helpful for advancing your progress.

Being patient is crucial throughout the process because self-improvement on any scale might take a long time. There are assistance programmes and templates available for those who feel they need a helping hand with any of the steps that were just listed. A variety of academic institutions or professional counsellors and tutors provide courses and seminars that focus on developing communication skills. Similar to this, there are numerous online communication tests that allow the individual to assess their strengths and weaknesses.

Following the leap and determining how to improve communication abilities, there are a few straightforward recommendations to help the individual through this illuminating process; - When speaking, make sure to maintain a steady and appropriate pace, use pauses when necessary, and strive to pronounce words clearly to prevent stuttering.

- When speaking, pay attention to using the appropriate volume, suitable tone, and volume changes when necessary for effect.

- Prepare for speaking engagements or parties. Take the opportunity to brush up on names and background information in advance if you frequently experience breakdowns or prolonged pauses in these situations. Practice asking yourself questions and then responding to them. For instance, ask yourself, "How have you been?" What have you been doing? and then look in the mirror. Recognize the context of the engagement; a formal agreement mandates a different communication style than an informal one, thus these skills may need to be applied differently.

CHAPTER TWO

The Art of Listening

We talk a great deal about what you are supposed to say when introducing MPM to others. We haven't discussed listening all that much. We're doing this because being a good listener is just as important as knowing what to say, if not more so. How are you going to know the right things to say to someone if you don't know where they are really coming from? That resulted from hearing!

Being an expert at listening will put you ahead of 90% of people in business. Do you understand how to truly listen? You should spend 20% of your conversational time asking and responding to questions. The remaining 80% should be spent listening to what the other person is saying and refraining from speaking.

More can be learned via listening than by speaking. Talk, and you lose. You win if you listen.

Many people who are working to build a business do a lot of telling and selling. They spend a lot of time promoting their business and products rather than engaging in conversation and learning more about the true concerns of the prospective clients. If you just listen, your prospect will tell you everything you need to know.

Learn to read body language. Learn how to assess a person's energy. If you know how to do it, you can learn everything you want to know about someone in the first minute.

Prospects enjoy feeling listened to. The person feels special when they are listened to. Are you a good reader or do you interrupt to make yourself feel better? Most people do not have a listening ear. When they discover that, it allows the person who is listening to them access to their mind. Listen without condemnation or criticism. It will instil a level of confidence in you in your contacts that will free their minds. The key to creating a valuable business relationship is listening.

If you don't read carefully, you'll pass up wonderful possibilities. Developing your listening skills is essential to creating a successful MPM business.

When you are speaking to someone, really listen to them. Don't think about what you're going to say next. Make sure you pay attention to what the other person is saying and not just what you expect to hear. There is typically a difference in terminology. You'll need to educate yourself in order to master the art of listening.

Concentrate. Don't focus solely on what they are saying. Observe their body language. What are those eyes saying? What are they omitting to say? That will only reveal to you a small portion of what they are saying. Lenticular below the surface. Respond positively. Affirmative listening is listening for, not just listening to, something.

You are listening to learn what you need to know. Positive listening truly links you to the person you are listening to.

There are many excellent books about listening. Get one of those now. Study it. Examine it. Make it a part of yourself. It will assist you in building your business as well. It will benefit you in every aspect of your life, including every relationship.

Utilize questions. Say something like:

Can you elaborate on that?

Whoa, what do you mean by that?

Tell me more!

Developing the skill of listening requires a commitment to change. Making a commitment to truly pay attention to the person you are listening to is what it means. They will inform you of what you need to know.

You already have a good idea of whether you are a good reader or not. Just be honest with yourself. Get started if there is a tonne of room for improvement. Your future is at stake!

There is more to listening than meets the eye—or, better yet, the ear. Listening involves more than just hearing what the other person says; it also involves understanding what they are saying on a deeper level and responding appropriately.

The inability to listen effectively leads to numerous communication breakdowns, wounded feelings, and misunderstandings. If we study and master the art of listening, our relationships and interactions with other people will be much more fruitful and fulfilling. For reading is a form of art all on its own. There are some considerations to keep in mind in order to develop your listening skills.

1. Never disrupt. It is both impolite and well-mannered to interrupt someone who is still speaking. Let him finish speaking after which you should make your mark. Your kindness and patience will be appreciated.

2. Pay attention to what is being said rather than just hearing it. The distinction between hearing and listening is substantial. The information enters one ear of hearing and frequently exits the other. When we read, we allow

the words to sink in more deeply. We make an effort to visualise what the other person is saying in our minds' eye. Therefore, listening requires focus and full attention. While hearing requires no effort, listening does.

3. Be impartial. Try to maintain an open mind toward what is being said and maintain personal space. judgments directed at you. Acceptance and tolerance of other people's opinions are not only admirable virtues, but they also enable the other person to speak freely without worrying about what you will think of him or her.

4. Attempt to comprehend on a deeper level. Listening is not simply about taking in the facts, storey, or opinion; it is also about making an effort to understand the other person's emotional message. Perhaps he or she needs your encouragement or support when they want to let go of some teams. People are frequently only seeking a sympathetic ear. The genuine listener will happily accept it.

5. Words are not as loud as silence. This is one of the keys to effective listening. The best listeners are those who do it in silence. Our mind or ego frequently assumes that we must respond with words, although this is untrue. Even if there are times when words are necessary, most of the time by remaining silent, we make it possible for the other speaker to say what he wants to say. Our presence gives the other person the peace and confidence to tell their

storey in its most comprehensive form, which benefits them both.

Last but not least, when we learn how to listen to others, we also learn how to listen to ourselves. If we practise meditation and go deep within, we will find an inner voice filled with wisdom that can lead and guide us in our outer lives. Spiritual teacher Sr. Chinmoy explains as follows: "The inner voice is both the man's true friend and guiding light. If a man looks deep inside, the inner voice will instruct him on what to do. How do we select the inner voice? We have to mediate early in the morning in order to select the inner voice.

We have faith in you!

The Art of Listening - How to Improve Your Listening Skills in 3 Easy Steps

You know you need to work on your listening skills when you no longer seem to be able to take instructions properly. Or when your coworker knocks you out with a rolled-up copy of yesterday's paper because she's been calling your name for five minutes and you haven't heard a word.

The art of listening is really simple to re-learn unless you have a severe ear infection or are actually losing your hearing. I advise you to re-learn because you used to be such a good reader. That is, go back to when you were in a similar state.

How then do you develop the art of listening? Try these steps on your own!

Step 1: Engage in Active Learning.

We take for granted having ears and the capacity to hear. We believe that just because we can hear what our employer is saying, it follows that we comprehend the message in its entirety.

The reality is more often than not the exact opposite. You'd be astonished at how easily the most mundane of things can distract us. Your supervisor may inform you of a crucial detail regarding the project when you are thinking about how your jeans fit at the time.

You need to get in the habit of actively listening in order to avoid distractions. Listen to the words and try to understand how they relate to you, rather than merely hearing them. Consciously forcing oneself to listen will prevent your mind from wandering as frequently.

Step 2: Reinforce The Message.

For people who struggle with concentration, listening can be difficult. One way to improve your listening skills is to mentally repeat the message while the speaker speaks.

This is comparable to the method of taking notes as the teacher explains the lecture. Nobody is aware of this clever trick. You are less likely to forget the message later if you repeatedly reinforce it in your mind.

Third step: Don't interrupt.

Even if you have something to say, the act of listening compels you to hold it until the speaker is through. You will be able to hear everything clearly in this way.

Not only do interruptions affect the speaker, but the listener as well. Always have a pen and paper with you if you're concerned about forgetting your own reminders. This way, you may write down any questions you have and remember to ask them once the speaker has finished speaking.

If you're ready to practise your talents, mastering the art of listening is quite simple. I'm cheering for you.

Have You Mastered the Art of Listening?

Don't you just love folks who listen to what you have to say? And don't you get annoyed by those who simply ignore what you have to say? We've all encountered both types, and the best way to deal with them is to educate oneself. Right? If you want to change others, start with analysing and improving yourself, don't you think? Have you developed a mastery of listening? Yes, learning is an art that must be perfected, just like anything else in life.

I am aware of several people close to me who, regrettably, suffer from an overly congested mind with perceived beliefs and thoughts about the outside world. As a result, they constantly have internal conversation going on. When I speak to them, I can tell by the look in their eyes and the way they respond to me that they did not hear a word I said because they were already formulating their own ideas about what they wanted to hear me say based on their preconceived notions and understanding or lack thereof of the situation at hand. There is therefore no other way for me to approach them than to shout at them and request that they stop and listen.

This usually shocks them for a split second, knocking them out of their internal monologue recording. Then, miracles might occur, causing them to actually pay attention for a minute before returning to their internal, self-serving monologue recording. Sound complicated? How about this then? I'm speaking to someone whose mind is already occupied with composing their response even as I speak to them, so they have already decided what to say regardless of what I say!

You must be completely present in the moment, fully focused on the here and now, forgetting about oneself, and possess an open, receptive mind in order to hear, receive, and process the information being conveyed to you in order to truly listen to someone speaking to you.

Focus and concentration are essential for effective listening. It doesn't matter if you're listening to a friend, family member, presentation, video, or radio broadcast. When you are truly interested, you either listen fully or partially while your mind is preoccupied with other ideas, or you completely switch off and fail to hear what is being said as it recedes into the background. It is even possible to go through all three stages while listening to a radio or having a lengthy conversation with a person you know well.

With all of today's technology and everyone's nose buried in their smartphones or anything else, it's difficult for people to even talk to one another, let alone listen to what others have to say. I have no idea how teenagers communicate these days or whether anyone is paying attention to anyone else at all. Imagine this scenario; we frequently see it in movies! It occurs even in the best of families! Both parents are rushing to get to work, the kids are eating a quick breakfast before heading off to school, and one of the kids is trying to get the attention of the mother or father about a problem. However, no one is listening because everyone is too busy rushing around to pay attention to the problem-solving child. The same thing occurs between couples as well. Everyone appears to be so preoccupied with work that nobody has time to even listen to anyone!

If you want to have a good relationship with your partner, parent, daughter, son, mother-in-law, and boss, as well as with your coworkers, neighbours, and everyone else you speak to, and you want to be remembered for it, read on. It's time to concentrate on measuring the Art of Listening if you want to be remembered as a "good" or "authentic" person who genuinely cared and listened. One of the most crucial life skills to possess is this one. Begin reading and collecting the awards that will be bestowed upon you.

Here are some tips to guide you along the way:

Maintain an open mind as you develop. Closed minds have a way of tagging.

Expand your mind and unclutter it. Your life is messed up by cracked minds.

Allow people to express themselves without interfering. Respecting others will earn you their respect.

Even when you disagree, show compassion and understanding. People will listen to what you have to say after that.

No matter how inferior you may find someone to be, never insult or disparage them. Encourage instead that this brings out the best in individuals, and you'll win some admirers.

Good communication involves both speaking clearly to convey yourself and listening intently to what others have to say. Make an effort to develop your listening skills and watch your relationships blossom.

CHAPTER THREE

Public Speaking Skills: Public Speaking Fear Comes From Perceived Failure

Like any other skill, public speaking requires practise, and the more success you have, the more self-confidence in public speaking you will develop. The more failures, or perceived failures, you have, the more fear of public speaking you are likely to have. The nervousness or anxiety you have when you speak in public is normal, but experiencing that fear for the rest of your life is definitely not.

Where does Public Speaking Fear Come From?

Think about any skill you have acquired during your life. For example, you didn't leave the womb knowing how to ride a bike, drive a car, play a musical instrument, or use a smartphone. The first time you tried any of these activities, you likely felt some type of discomfort or nervosity. The key to developing self-confidence in these abilities, or any skill, is having some type of success where you were raised.

But if the early stages of skill development are plagued by failures, the confidence in oneself will diminish. For example, if someone who had never driven a car before gets behind the wheel by himself or herself (without a teacher or passenger), there is a good chance that this first experience won't go very well. If the first attempt to drive is on a freeway, then that fear, just like public speaking fear, is likely to be really strong. At the end of the drive, the person might say, "I never, ever want to experience that again!" The fear will grow if a boss forces the person to attempt the skill years later.

Public Speaking Skill is Developed through Success

Start with something less risky to learn a skill better. In the previous car example, the majority of people begin in a parking lot with a parent or a child. The new driver may switch to making right-hand turns around a neighbourhood once their confidence has grown a little. Next, switch to left-turns. Then, perhaps, enter a more busy traffic area. The freeway comes last. If you want to develop public speaking abilities and eliminate public speaking anxiety, you should use a similar strategy.

Start with something less scary, such as speaking up in the staff meeting. Input on ideas or problems is typically sought for by managers or executives at staff meetings. Develop the habit of speaking out at least once during these discussions. Next, offer to volunteer to present a report on a project at a staff meeting. Once you feel more at ease with these kind of public speaking opportunities, try something riskier. Maybe ask questions as an audience member in a larger presentation. Remember that just as you had more nerves as you progressed through how to drive, the parking lot felt genuinely safe when you arrived at the freeway. The same thing will occur with public speaking fear. As you begin to experience The more complicated the presentations, the more natural they become.

Public Speaking Coach can Speed Up Your Confidence Growth

Like your parents or the instructor who taught you how to drive a car step-by-step, a good public speaker can cut a lot of time off the length of your learning curve. For example, it might take you some time to learn how to park correctly if you went to the parking lot for the first time while driving. The hardest part would be that you would have very little context to compare your skill with, making it difficult for you to recognise when you are performing well. That thought you would be having in the back of your mind would make you nauseous. One of the most crucial aspects of cooking is having someone tell you when you performed the skill correctly. By the way, you are not required to search for a professional business coach or public speaker. Simply ask someone who you believe stands out among the group and presents themselves well to watch you and give you feedback. Many toasting clubs use this style of blending.

However, if you don't have much time, you could choose to hire a professional coach. A good public speaking coach may help you develop public speaking abilities in a day or two that would typically take most people years to develop, as well as prevent you from forming bad habits. For example, when I was in my twenties, I wanted to learn how to play golf. I bought some inexpensive second-hand clubs and went to the municipal golf course because I was broke. After a few months, I started to feel pretty good, although I had a terrible lump that hurt my range just a little bit. When I played with friends, I was always two or three strokes behind the group. Actually, I just decided that golf wasn't my game and stopped playing. Years later, I tried picking it back up and went to a golf course close to my house. I questioned him about how long it would take me to reach competitiveness. He said, "It might have taken a few months if you had reached out to me in the beginning, but it will be much harder now. "When I asked him why, he explained to me that I had developed a habit of turning my body in a different direction to correct the problem because of my laziness. I just changed my aiming point over the years because I knew my ball would drift. My body had grown accustomed to that swing, therefore I had to unlearn that habit before I could relearn a more appropriate swing.

I may have saved myself some time and fruit if I had simply practised getting feedback early on from someone who could already do what I wanted to do. You can speak in public as well. Look for a person who has already conquered their fear and let them speak to you. Your chew will help you eliminate your public speaking fear far more quickly.

The Importance Of Public Speaking Skills

People frequently mistakenly believe that public speaking abilities are unimportant or that they will never be asked to speak in public, which is why they choose not to enlist in any public speaking programmes. Truth be told, more often than not, it is these people who become tongue-tied and go into a complete breakdown when faced with the possibility that they will be asked to present a topic in public, even one that they are intimately familiar with.

Some people do not place a high value on having good public speaking abilities because they believe that such abilities are only appropriate for those working in sales or marketing. It is untrue. Good public speaking abilities are also a sign of good communication abilities, and having good communication abilities is necessary for any career, unless you are the only person in the entire office. For instance, if you are looking for a new job, or any job at all, you will likely need to go for an interview. The interviewer does not just assess you based on your qualifications; they also consider your ability to communicate, both spoken and unspoken, as part of the decision-making process as to whether you will be accepted or not. If you are a college student, your ability to provide a strong public speaking performance will also be regularly tested. A good example of this would be the various class presentations you must complete throughout the semester, and the grading criteria will almost certainly include a component for "clearness of delivery." Lack of effective public speaking abilities can only disadvantage you since if you can't communicate with your audience clearly, it's as if you've never learned the subject at all.

This is one of the possible explanations for why many ideas by some of the smartest people on the internet are only discovered many years after their passing. One of the possible explanations is that, despite their great intelligence and ability to write really helpful information, they just lack the ability to effectively communicate to big groups of people using public speaking techniques.

Public speaking abilities are not only used in situations where you must address a sizable group of people. Public speaking and communication skills are interrelated, therefore if you improve your public speaking skills, you also invariably improve your interpersonal communication skills with your coworkers and family.

Therefore, if you ever get the chance to practise public speaking or acquire public speaking skills, seize the opportunity. Pick up your course material and go for it whether you're in class, at work, or in any other setting where you need to deliver a message to an audience. Public speaking is a skill, and the more you use and practise it, the better you will get. There are many public speaking audiobooks or how-to books available for you to learn from whether you want to hone your public speaking abilities or even if you are just getting started.

By developing strong public speaking abilities, you will have an advantage over those who don't.

10 Public Speaking Skills

How proficient are you at public speaking? Have you tested your public speaking abilities?

If you want to evaluate public speaking, you must evaluate your public speaking abilities. There are plenty of skills need for a discourse. These skills are a crucial component of public speaking and are particularly crucial in persuasion. How do you rate yourself in just 10 of the skills?

You can find the skill and a brief explanation of what it is or requires in the paragraphs that follow.

Informative to the Audience

It requires the crucial "what's in it for me" factor in order to be informative to the audience. Additionally, it must go beyond mere facts and data. The information must be managed so that the audience can use it.

Know the Make Up of Your Audience

This seems obvious, but it is frequently overlooked. For instance, you would anticipate speaking to doctors differently from those without a background in health care. Whatever information doctors deal with online, they prefer the common version, which they will share with their patients. Be aware of the best way for the audience to receive the material you present.

Introductions that Capture Attention

The key that unlocks the door of the mind so that what you say could be listened to is the introduction. It is crucial that the words chosen and the way they are utilised be effective in grabbing the listener's attention. Although it may seem like one of the more basic public speaking skills, this is actually one of the most crucial.

Accurate Pronunciation

Imagine listening to a fantastic speaker who continuously mispronounces words. Will you wonder if it's because he didn't know? How credible is everything else he has to say if he didn't know?

Words Clearly Spoken

Clarity is essential, much as pronouncing words. What you're all doing could be acceptable while we're with friends, but when speaking into a microphone, it might be annoying to the audience. Lack of clarity can produce sound that you wouldn't want to utilise in public. Even worse, slurred speech is a sign and symptom of a stroke. Someone might dial 911 not just to rescue the audience but also (as far as the stroke is concerned) to rescue you.

This is one of the public speaking abilities we might use for reward, but it might also land us in trouble.

Fluency

Fluency refers to how quickly your thoughts flow. The language that is being spoken sounds more like a terrifying whole than like a collection of fragmented, little thoughts that have been quickly put together.

Word Whiskers

In addition to the commonly used words, "and now" would be the more appropriate phrase. Or occasionally just plan "now." ' Speaking Spanish, a common word for whisker is "therefore." ' There are other other word-whikers, as you are aware. ' In certain instances, using them only once may be acceptable. Using them repeatedly is annoying and distracting to the listener, as you now know.

Pausing

Pausing can be done for emphasis or for effect. It is a speaker skill that is frequently underutilised. Use moderate emphasis to highlight a certain word or section of the thought. Before making a firm statement or emphasising the statement, pause. No less than one second, and no more than three, please. One of the more challenging public speaking skills to master and be natural is this.

Sense stress

Putting the right emphasis on the right words or the right segment of a talk requires practise. Inexperienced speakers will often be observed adding unnecessary stress to more than one section of a speech or more than one section of a shared idea.

Enthusiastic Presentation

Did you know that there are two types of Muslims? One is a put-on or Pan American smile, and the other is a genuine smile. Enthusiasm might be similar to the same. It might seem forced or genuine. For great speaking, mastering the real is crucial. Developing this skill along with other speaking abilities will make a talk come to life.

These are only 10 of the many speaker skills. There are many more. To master public speaking, one must first become a skilled public speaker. The last rehearsal will be place in front of an audience. Learn them, practise them, and once proficient, you will have acquired accurate measurement.

Managing the Fear of Speaking

Public speaking abilities are crucial for you as a leader. A good public speaker may excite, inspire, and alter people with only one speech.

Public speaking is actually a very useful ability to have when you consider that businesses actually try to use large bonuses and pay increases to try to motivate their employees.

By learning how to speak effectively to inspire and encourage people, you can save thousands of dollars compared to trying to motivate your team or employees with money (which, by the way, is a lousy method of motivation).

Jerry Sened stated, "According to most studies, public speaking is people's top dread. Death is numbered two. The number two is death. Does that make sense? This suggests that, for the average person, attending a funeral is preferable to performing the eulogy. "Now that's amusing, but it might be true!

You've probably had some experience with public speaking, and you're just downright frightened of it. The idea of having to speak in front of people and having every action and word evaluated by others just makes you feel uncomfortable!

Given the advantages of effective public speaking, it is crucial that you learn how to control your anxiety before speaking in front of an audience.

First, comprehend what the fears are.

Common fears experienced by presenters

Some of the common fears experienced by presenters include the worry of seeming foolish, the fear that the content is inadequate, the dread of being examined, and the fear of the unknown.

But all of these fears may be summed up in one universal fear: the sense of being inadequate.

In essence, it indicates that you feel insufficient and that the thought of speaking in front of everyone makes you feel as though you are being watched from every angle as you stand up there.

Everyone in the audience makes you feel as though every step you take and every word you say will be scrutinised by the people who are listening to you.

Those are scary thoughts, aren't they?

What? You're not alone, I tell you. They are widespread among those who have spoken in front of audiences as well.

But you are unique. You must learn how to overcome these fears as a leader so that they do not turn you into a slave.

Techniques for public speaking

Recognize that it is customary for public speakers and presenters to be reticent.

Recognize that it's not only you who is experiencing it. I experienced the same thing. And before each presenter gets up to talk, he or she has a certain amount of anxiety.

I recall a speaker who once shared with the congregation that after having been a preacher for 25 years, he still feels a little uneasy speaking to a crowd of thousands.

Focus on the task that hand

Adlai Stevenson said, "It's hard to lead a cavalry charge if you think you look funny on a horse."

People frequently become nervous on stage because they are preoccupied with thoughts of themselves, how they appear, and how their words sound.

Stop thinking about yourself if you notice that's all you're thinking about! Your heart ought to belong to your people. Concentrate on the current message.

What is it that you want your team to learn? What is the message that you need to convey? If you put your attention on these things, you'll discover that your words come to you easily.

I've been at the point where I've been quite hesitant to speak out because for the majority of the time, I was just considering whether my message is good enough for my team. However, you just have to let that go, consider what they need to hear, and say it.

Pass it by. Public speaking will seem natural to you once you stop thinking about yourself and start thinking about the people you are guiding.

Speaking from your heart

What is on your mind? What is burning inside of you that you want to tell your team? This is one thing that no public speaking course can teach you how to do.

To inspire others, you must have a clear vision of the future and lead your team in that direction.

In a world of social conventions, you must have the courage to speak up for the future you want to create and dedicate your life to making it a reality.

I personally have not taken a course on public speaking techniques, yet I have been able to give moving speeches using only my heart.

People have told me in their feedback that I've really motivated them to want to keep serving their community.

Since I had only drawn my speech out of my head a few hours prior, I must admit that I was shocked by the impact it made.

But it was at that point that I realised you can only make a powerful speech with your heart, not with someone else's script or any techniques.

What is inside your heart? Share it.

These are just a few techniques you may use to manage your fear of speaking; search for more articles on public speaking techniques and leadership strategies you can use to become a more persuasive, inspirational speaker.

CHAPTER FOUR

COMMUNICATION SHOULD BE NATURAL – SO WHY DO WE FIND IT CHALLENGING?

21 Days of Effective Communication skiils

Day 1: Listen

Before you even consider how you will respond to other people, you need to improve your listening abilities. Have you ever spoken with someone whose body is present but whose mind is absent? It's fruitful, isn't it?

Poor communicators believe that "listening" is simply the act of patiently waiting for their turn to speak while mentally composing their response. This is a major error. Reading is much more than that; it gives someone else the chance to express their views, foster emotional stability, and demonstrate empathy.

Today, you will learn the fundamentals of excellent listening before engaging in an exercise that will enable you to put these ideas into practise.

Giving someone else the chance to express what's on their mind is important in and of itself, but listening is more than that. Reading is also the first step toward personal improvement.

One of the most influential psychologists of the 20th century, Carl Rogers, noted that when someone gives us the chance to talk about what has happened to us and how we feel about it, we begin to realise the best way to change our ideas and behaviours.

Although getting advice from someone else can be helpful, we are more likely to change for the better if we solve our own problems. One of the most effective methods to accomplish this is to be able to speak freely to an understanding audience.

Give your conversation partner the space they require if they ramble if their ideas don't seem to make sense. Before putting a plan into action, they might want to consult with a number of other people, or they might want to handle the situation on their own. Try not to become irritated! Give others the same patience you would like to receive in return.

Top tips that will make you an outstanding listener

1. Urge them to continue talking by using non-intrusive verbal and non-verbal cues. "Uh huh" and "I see" are examples of brief, unobtrusive cues that encourage further clarification. Silence is also acceptable since occasionally, someone needs a few minutes to gather their thoughts before continuing the talk. Give them space.

2. Allow them to continue speaking until they run out of breath: When I learned how to listen properly, I was amazed to discover that many people desperately want someone to pause and listen to what they have to say. This is especially true if they are angry, upset, or need to solve a problem.

One of the most important, fundamental, and difficult listening skills of all is to remain silent and let the other person hold the floor. When you are dealing with someone who is furious or frustrated, they won't be able to think properly until they have let everything out of their mind.

3. Avoid taking on the role of an armour psychologist: To some extent, everyone is a psychologist. We all like to come up with our own theories on why certain people are constantly angry, why our cousin always chooses men who treat her badly, etc. Analyze right away at your own pace.

When someone shares important information with you, avoid asking them about their personal motivations or the reasons behind their actions. You'll at least come across as a little nosy. Your conversation partner will likely feel resentful and angry at first. At you. 4. Never interrupt with unwelcome advice: Even if you've had the same difficulties or situations as someone else, refrain from sharing your thoughts or solutions unless specifically requested. Few things are more annoying than unwelcome advice or suggestions.

Refrain from telling them that you understand exactly what they are going through. To put it simply, you don't. Two people may share a similar experience, but due to differences in personality, upbringing, and past life events, they won't feel the same emotions.

Go ahead and give your opinion if your conversation partner requests it, but be sure to judge their response. Continue if they seem open to your feedback. Whether they begin to turn away, cross their arms, or otherwise indicate that your advice is not welcome or helpful, stop and ask if they would like you to continue.

Keep in mind that no one is obligated to follow your recommendations. Set your focus on one side. After you have contributed, the other person must plan their next step. Furthermore, they could not be telling the whole storey, so they will need to take other factors and considerations into account while formulating a plan of action.

5. Rephrase someone else's words without repeating them backwards: You may have heard that repeating someone else's words back to them indicates that you have been paying attention. This is accurate—to a point. There is a fine line between expressing your understanding of someone and quoting them exactly.

I'll give an example to clarify the concept. Let's say your friend said the following:

"I've been feeling quite lonely lately. It seems like my family doesn't care what I'm doing or whether I'm even happy."

Here are two potential replies. Which do you think would help your friend feel truly heard, and which would make them feel really annoyed?

"So, you feel like they aren't giving you much attention right now?"

Or

"You've been feeling lonely lately, and like your family doesn't care what you're doing?"

The second response demonstrates that you heard the real words, but it also sounds extremely strange! Your companion might be confused if she is speaking to a parrot instead of a human being. I prefer the first response because it reflects an understanding of both the words' meaning and the words themselves.

6. Review your presumptions. We all have a tendency to see the world through the prism of our personal preferences and experiences. For instance, if you are close to your parents and love speaking to your mother on the phone once a week, you are likely to be upset on someone else's behalf if they inform you that their own mother is seriously ill.

However, if your conversation partner has a distant relationship with their parents, they usually won't anticipate a particularly empathic response. In actuality, they can feel uneasy due to your empathy.

What is the lesson here? Do not project your own feelings onto other people. Let them explain to you what a situation means to them personally. You should never instruct someone on how to feel. Recognize that everyone has unique characteristics and that no two people will react exactly the same way in the same situation.

Use it in your daily life.

Your task for today is to call a friend or relative that you haven't seen or spoken to in a while, and then take advantage of the opportunity to practise active listening during the chat.

You only need to try a 20-minute chat; you don't need to be on the phone for hours. As you inquire about their recent activities, make an effort to listen attentively. You might be shocked to learn how frequently you fall into negative reading habits. Reread this chapter thereafter and evaluate your performance honestly.

The workout has a nice side benefit as well. You can establish and strengthen your relationship with your buddy or relative by calling them. Think back to the last time someone unexpectedly called you and genuinely wanted to know how you were doing. Good, didn't it feel? You felt valuable. The person you call will likely feel the same way. Maybe you should make it a habit to call them frequently.

Day 2: Count The Number Of Times You Interrupt Other People

What would be the most unpleasant communication habit you could think of? Although there are many possibilities, most of us agree that being disturbed is among the most upsetting. Today, you will consider how frequently you interrupt others before working to give your conversation partners the time and space they require.

It is simple to enter people. For instance, if you participate in a contentious discussion, you might want to jump right in to assert your voice. If you are passionate about an idea, your enthusiasm may come out on the surface.

But therein lays the difficulty. Even if your thoughts are great, if you interrupt, your conversation partner won't be able to give them the attention they need. You are insinuating that your thoughts and ideas are more significant than theirs by your interruption. You are aware from personal experience that interruptions cause your train of thought to divert.

Additionally, violations might make someone feel mistreated. Right? If someone values you and your opinions, they should at least have the decency to allow you to end your speech. Apply the same principle when actively listening to others.

Interrupting can completely destroy your chances of forming a good relationship with someone else, and that is not an exaggeration. They will begin to distance themselves from you if they believe that you are more interested in seeing them from your personal point of view than in getting to know them.

Here's how to break the habit of interruption:

1. Set goals and give yourself rewards: Decide on a tiny reward as a sufficient motivator and set a reasonable objective. For instance, you may promise yourself that if you manage to interrupt people less than ten times

throughout the day, you'll pick up your favourite magazine or candy bar on the way home.

2. Static symbols: Sometimes the simplest solutions are the best! I keep a tiny sticky note on my computer monitor to remind me not to disturb other people. It has a patch of a closed mouth immediately below an ear. When I'm on the phone or webcam, I glance at it. It reminds me that in order to grow my relationships and my business, I must allow others to talk.

3. Outline any points you wish to make in advance: While you cannot take notes during an impromptu encounter, you may bring a list to a scheduled meeting. It's simpler to refrain from interrupting when you are aware that your main arguments are strategically bolded on paper.

You can also make notes of your thoughts during other people's speeches in formal meetings. When they're done, you can refer to your notes and request clarification.

4. Keep in mind that your presence has just as much power as your voice: Nobody enjoys a showoff or someone who seems to enjoy the sound of their own voice. On the other hand, everyone respects someone who listens to others and uses caution while expressing their own opinions. If the idea of continuing is present terrifies you, keep in mind that your inclination may have its roots in a feeling of insecurity.

Some long-term disrupters experience pressure to demonstrate that they have original thoughts or have merited a spot in the room. Does this sound familiar? If so, your habit may be more than just a bothersome obstacle. It may be time to examine any lingering feelings of insecurity and deal with them, either on your own or with the assistance of a licenced therapist.

5. Exercise biting your tongue: Here, the expression "bite your tongue" might be taken literally. Put your tongue between your teeth when you feel the need to interrupt. The event will serve as a constant reminder not to butt in.

Cultural differences

The advice I've assumed in this chapter that you and others around you have grown up in a culture that interprets interruptions as a sign of rudeness. Most Americans would agree that it's polite to wait until someone else has finished speaking before responding.

However, it's important to keep in mind that people perceive disruptions differently depending on their culture. For instance, some cultures view interruptions and cross-talk as normal.

For two specific examples, people of Italian heritage frequently view interruptions as acceptable methods of expressing interest in a topic. Meanwhile, those raised in Japanese culture frequently hold the belief that it is acceptable to impose on someone in order to ask for clarification.

Consider the potential of a cultural difference when you encounter someone who seems especially quick to interrupt. Asking someone to recount their family's history is inappropriate, but simply being aware of these differences can help you remain composed and patient.

You can bridge the gap by making an explicit request such as, "I've got something really important to say and don't want to forget anything, so if you have any questions, could you please save them for the end?"

Put It Into Practice

Today's exercise is actually really simple, or at least it is in theory. Count how many times you interrupt other people in all of your talks, then use the tips above to stop it. You should make an effort to speak with at least three people. Even better if you can do this while working as a team.

The first time I performed this exercise, I was shocked to find that I had trouble even letting others finish their sentences. Although I didn't mean to be rude or obnoxious, my conversation partners must have been extremely frustrated.

Without making an effort to keep myself in check, I still find myself interrupting others far too frequently. Although it's a difficult habit to overcome, your friends and family will appreciate it. Who knows, if you master the art of keeping your mouth shut, you might learn something new.

Day 3: Become An Inclusive Communicator

We all have our own opinions when it comes to politics and social issues. One thing, however, that most of us can agree on is that everyone deserves to be treated with respect, regardless of their background or unique personal characteristics. You will learn about the value of indirect communication today.

What exactly is "inclusive communication"?

In essence, a good indirect communicator takes care not to alienate or offend a whole group of people based solely on their particular contributions. They don't base their judgments on an individual's traits. Include communication skills and a diversity of values.

The importance of measuring this skill has grown in the twenty-first century. Due to globalisation, people from all backgrounds now work and interact together. Organize together. Included communication fosters toxic relationships between individuals and even improves business performance. According to research, there is a positive correlation between gender diversity, ethnic diversity, and organisational profitability.

Tips for inclusive communication

1. Avoid emphasising a characteristic unless it is absolutely required to do so: For illustration, imagine that you are informing your team that a member of another department has been scheduled to collaborate with them on a new project. This worker, a man named Sam, just so happens to be gay.

Saying "Sam, the gay guy from Department X, will be joining us on Monday" would not be appropriate. Sam's sexual orientation has no bearing on his employment, so bringing attention to this characteristic is not necessary.

2. Never infer a person's gender or sexual orientation: Choose gender-neutral terms if at all possible. If your manager is leaving the company and you are unsure of who will take over, for instance, it is more appropriate to refer to potential candidates as "they" rather than "he" or "she" until a permanent replacement has been chosen.

Never assume that someone is heterosexual. It's preferable to use words like "partner" or "significant other" rather than "boyfriend," "wife," and so on.

3. If you need to discuss someone's ability, use neutral language: It is true that many people with impairments suffer as a result, however it is presumptuous to say

things like "Peter suffers from epilepsy" or "Mary is affected with schizophrenia."

4. Concentrate on a person rather than any impairments they might have: Don't define people based on their conditions or traits. For instance, it is preferable to say "Pat has depression" as opposed to "Pat is a depressive" or "Pat is depressed."

5. Avoid reinforcing stereotypes: Making assumptions about someone based on their nationality, ethnicity, or other characteristics is offensive because it demonstrates a lack of respect for their unique talents and personality. This principle holds true even for positive stereoscopic types.

For instance, it would be inappropriate to suggest that Chinese people naturally make good accountants since "Asians are so adept at math" if you met a Chinese accountant.

6. Respect race and ethnicity by capitalising words correctly in written communication: For example, the terms "Native American," "Black," and "Torres Strait Islanders" should always be capitalised. When in doubt, look up the term in a dictionary or consult a reliable online resource.

7. Consider the context: Keep in mind that it is sometimes appropriate for group members to use words that would

be objectionable to outsiders. For instance, some LGBT+ community members refer to themselves as "sueer."

However, this word is typically regarded as offensive if used by a heterosexual person, and not all LGBT+ people first accept it. If in doubt, it is best to avoid using any "loaded" expressions that have historically been used to insult or belittle others. [10]

Avoid patronising individuals or groups of people. If you have a disability, you may have heard someone refer to you as "brave" or "inspiring" for carrying out routine daily duties like cleaning your house, going to work, or exercising at the gym.

I have a cousin who uses a cane after suffering injuries in a car accident several years ago. Many well-meaning people have commended him for being "an inspiration." Their intentions are good, but my gut just feels oppressed. Do not assume that simply because someone has a disability, they want to be acknowledged for it!

Is open communication actually necessary?

I recognise that some people may consider inclusive communication to be "too politically correct." However, regardless of how you personally view the land, if you don't use inclusive communication, you could easily find yourself in trouble. For example, using sexist language in the workplace could get you into trouble with HR or give you a reputation as someone who doesn't keep up with modern etiquette.

Why making offensive jokes is bad even if you're "just kidding"

Over the years, I've encountered a small number of people who assert that making offensive jokes or stereotyping groups of people is acceptable as long as you don't actually hold harmful views.

But consider this: People who support harmful stereotypes and hold racist, sexist, or other offensive ideas would feel offended anytime they hear such "jokes."

This means that hatred of all kinds—including racism, sexism, and others—goes unchecked.

Make no jokes that rely on derogatory humour and let others know that you don't think them amusing.

Put It Into Practice

Exercise I

Do you express stereotypes, whether positive or negative, while discussing specific groups? The next time you participate in a discussion that includes a discussion about other people, think about whether your choice of words is respectful. Could you communicate more eloquently? Make a note of where and how you could enhance the next time around, if relevant.

Exercise II

Turn on the TV (or visit YouTube) and look for a programme that has a lot of dialect. Watch it for around 15 minutes. Are there any negative opinions or views held by those participating in the conversation concerning specific groups? Do you frequently encounter similar terminology in your interactions? If so, how would you contest it?

Day 4: How To Expand Your Vocabulary

If you can show off a broad vocabulary, you will be viewed more favourably in social situations. Most people consider a person has a higher level of education and intelligence when they can correctly use numerous words within the context of everyday conversation.

Understanding and appreciating difficult words and phrases puts a person at a real advantage, both personally and professionally. You will discover today why having a large vocabulary is a benefit and how to add more words to your personal dictionary.

Why your vocabulary really does make a difference

There is a connection between vocabulary and professional success. According to a study by linguist and education researcher Jonathan O'Conner, those who perform well on verbal aptitude tests are much more likely to hold high-level jobs.

This finding holds true even when gender, age, and academic level are taken into account.

[12] Even more intriguing, vocabulary test performance predicts success - it's not merely a byproduct of working in senior roles or coming into contact with educated people.

What is happening here, then? In a word, having a strong vocabulary is the best foundation for communication, and communication is the key to success. When you have more words available to you, you are in a better position. position to convey just the right message.

The more diverse your vocabulary, the more proficient you will be at articulating nuanced ideas and comprehending new lines of reasoning.

A person with a large vocabulary can adapt their oral and written communication to a variety of audiences, which enables them to develop productive relationships with others that allow them to flourish.

A large vocabulary also enables you to absorb information from complex sources, giving you the tools you need to advance your personal and professional abilities. For instance, if you are confident reading and comprehending high-level textbooks, you are more likely to gain from advanced education and training than people who can only recognise common words every day.

Your reading speed will also increase when you are familiar with complex words because you won't have to stop to look up a word. Obviously, right?

Here are a few strategies that will aid you:

1. Use a different word each day: Make it a habit to look up a new term every morning and then use it at some point during the day. If it's a very obscure word and you can't naturally incorporate it into a discussion, at the very least, inform someone that you just learned a fascinating new word and then explain what it means.

2. Use online games and apps to broaden your vocabulary: Numerous free applications and games have been created to aid users in learning new phrases. One of my favourites is Free Ride (freeride.com). It is a straightforward multiple-choice game that tests your vocabulary. The more questions you correctly answer, the trickier they get!

If you provide a false response, the website will point out your error. As an extra bonus, the site's creators donate a small sum of money to those in need for every correct response you provide. Popular apps that make learning new words simple are PowerVocab (vocabulary.com), 7

Little Words (7lttlw.com), and Words With Friends 2 (zynga.com).

3. Become a word enthusiast: Learning words in isolation will help you expand your vocabulary, but developing a deeper understanding of a word's structure and roots will put you in an excellent position to comprehend new words you come across in the future.

When learning a word for the first time, break it down into its component pieces.

For instance, the term "orthostatic" is defined as "relating to or produced by an upright posture," and if you split the word apart, you'll see that it's a combination of the terms "ortho" and "static," which both imply "concerning with bodies at rest." Understanding the definitions of prefixes and suffixes will you in your ability to interpret new words.

4. Read widely: This is the standard piece of advice for everyone who wants to sound knowledgeable and educated. Avoid reading the same books and magazines you always do. Challenge yourself by discovering new topics and reading text that is denser and more difficult.

Set aside at least 15 minutes per day for reading. In my opinion, there is no good reason not to read because it will improve your vocabulary and make you a more well-rounded person who can communicate with just about everyone.

5. If you are unsure of the meaning of a word, inquire. When someone uses a word that you are unfamiliar with, it's normal to feel embarrassed, but it's also a golden opportunity to learn something new.

If someone attempts to make you feel inferior because you don't know what a word means, then that is their issue. At the very least, make a note of the word and look it up later in your dictionary if you really can't ask at the moment.

Put It Into Practice

Exercise I

Today You must learn five new words and incorporate them into your spoken or written communication.

Exercise II

Look over the apps and websites mentioned in this chapter and commit to using one of them for at least five minutes per day for a week.

Day 5: Swap "But" For "And," & Embrace "Yet"

Sometimes, the seemingly insignificant details can have a significant impact. Today, I'm going to focus on the terms "but", "and", and "yet," because the words we use influence not only how other people perceive us but also how we perceive ourselves.

When you practise positive communication, the world will start to seem more inviting. You'll start to perceive opportunities rather than problems, and other people will be drawn to your proactive, positive personality. You don't need to think these tips will work; just put them into action and observe the difference for yourself.

"But", "and", and positive communication

How often do you hear people say "but" statements? Here are a few examples:

"I'd love to go on vacation, but I'm scared of flying."

"I'd like to go back to school, but I don't have any free time." "I want to run a marathon, but I'm so out of shape."

Each of these claims attributes a specific explanation to a problem or situation. They claim they cannot travel because they are afraid of flying, they cannot attend school because they don't have any free time, they cannot run a marathon because they are out of shape, etc.

Most people don't realise that a typical "but" sentence is unnecessarily limiting and negative. This becomes more apparent if you remove "but" and then insert "and" in its place. Take the first example in the list above – "I'd love to go on vacation, but I'm scared to fly."

Swap “but” for “and” and you notice the difference immediately: “I’d love to go on vacation, and I’m scared to fly.”

The amended version implies that the speaker might actually be terrified of flying because they want to go on vacation. Although it's a small difference, it matters! It implies that the person has a want but also a problem that needs to be fixed, as opposed to a desire that will be thwarted by their problem.

When I first begin working with a client, I frequently observe that they repeatedly say the same old "but" phrases. They become our own personal narratives, justifications we accept without question. We take them at face value and assume that they are the absolute truth.

These ingrained views started to resemble a screenplay in certain ways. The more you repeat them, the more immersed you become in the role of someone who would love to change their life but is unable to do so because they are held back by a single outside force.

When I instruct my students to remove the word "but" and replace it with "and," I almost always observe a rapid change in their writing. This shift in perspective started to show in their expression within a short period of time. As students realise that how you frame a situation makes all the difference when coming up with answers to an issue, hope replaces desperation.

Another problem with using "but"

"But" can also make people defensive. Most of us automatically think that criticism or bad news is coming as soon as we hear that small phrase.

For instance, if you were to tell someone that you agree with them but prefer to utilise a different strategy, they would likely feel threatened and chastised. However, letting them know that you understand their perspective and would want to use a different strategy will usually elicit a more favourable response.

It suggests that even though you won't use their input, you value it. This technique creates a sense of closeness and mutual allegiance.

The power of "yet"

Simply putting "yet" on the end of a negative statement can transform its meaning.

Let's look at a few examples:

"I don't know enough about this topic to pass the exam."

"I don't know enough about this topic to pass the exam yet." "I can't get a girlfriend."

"I can't get a girlfriend yet."

“I just don’t earn enough money to buy a house.”

“I just don’t earn enough money to buy a house yet.”

The word "yet" conveys to both yourself and other people that you have not given up. You are aware that things could change. You may not know exactly how you will make these changes come to pass, but at least you are considering the idea. It immediately transforms you into a happier, more optimistic person, at least in the view of others.

This technology is not just effective in conversion. It works well when it comes to your own self-talk. It promotes a feeling of optimism and potential while still encouraging you to maintain reality. It acknowledges your current circumstance and issues while also emphasising that you are moving in the correct direction.

Put It Into Practice

There are two exercises for you to try today.

Exercise I

When you catch yourself saying something negative that contains the word "but," replace it with "and." Don't be surprised if your optimism proves to be harmful.

This one small adjustment will make you sound confident and upbeat. It will inspire others. Instead of trying this out in conversation, use it as a journaling exercise.

Give yourself five minutes to write down any "but" statements you've lately made. What happens if "and" is used in place of "but"? Personally, I feel less helpless in the face of my difficulties when I make this straightforward switch.

Exercise II

Take a "Yet Hunt." Every time you state something negatively or lament the fact that you lack a certain resource, add the word "yet" at the end. You may also subtly insert a "yet" at the conclusion of other people's sentences and observe how it alters their meaning. You could be tempted to start suggesting to others that they use "yet" more frequently, but this is best avoided unless you are certain that they value constructive criticism.

Day 6: Watch Your Pronouns

Unless you are correcting a monologue, you must always take your conversation partner's needs into account. Never tyre of them. Break this rule at your own risk. There is no use in expressing your opinions if no one is going to listen to them in the first place.

Do you enjoy talking about yourself? You are typical!

The average person would likely respond, "Me?" if you were to ask them if they enjoy talking about themselves and listening to their own voice. No, of course not. But let's face it, most of us enjoy talking about ourselves. In moderation, that is completely acceptable. You are leading your own life, therefore it makes sense that you would find your own experiences fascinating.

People who never reveal anything about themselves are also not seen as trustworthy. The best communicators understand how to balance self-deprecation with consideration for others.

Limit your "I"s

A fascinating research study conducted in 1988 at the University of California discovered a relationship between narcism and the frequency with which a person used the pronoun "I" over the course of a five-minute monologue. The subjects, 24 men and 24 women, were given the opportunity to speak for several minutes on a topic of their choosing.

Their monologues were videotaped, and the researchers then counted the instances in which each participant used first-person pronouns. The participants who performed better on the narcotics measures tended to use "I" more frequently.

Does this imply that "I" speak is a trustworthy narcotics indicator? Not exactly. Later research has revealed that there is truly no relationship between the two. What does this mean for those of us who want to leave a good first impression?

Although psychologists dispute on whether "I" talk is actually related to narcism, the average layperson picks up on it. In other words, a psychologist might conclude that using the pronoun "I" doesn't always indicate that you are narcissistic, but most people will. In conclusion, it is safe to say that refraining from using the singular pronoun "I" will benefit you.

When to use "I"

Too much "I" speaking will not win you any friends, but it is occasionally the right course of action. When you should use it is as follows:

1. When acting assertively: If you are standing up for your rights, using "I" creates a clear separation between you and the other person and enables you to express how the situation makes you feel.

Let's say your partner doesn't do their fair share of the domestic chores. It would be more effective to use "I" language to describe how their actions have made you feel rather than pointing out all of their flaws and demanding that they change right away.

Someone can challenge your interpretation of their actions, but they cannot challenge your feelings.

Statements beginning with "I" are less offensive than those that begin with "you."

To continue with the previous example, it would be preferable to say "You don't do anything, and the house is a complete mess!" as opposed to "I feel unappreciated when I get home to find that you haven't cleaned the kitchen after you promised to do so."

2. When you wish to introduce a potentially controversial viewpoint: If you're talking about a sensitive subject, like religion or politics, it's a good idea to let everyone in the audience know that you can respect other people's viewpoints. Your opinions are wholly unique and do not represent those of anyone else.

Avoid presenting your viewpoint as fact; instead, start it with a "I" to avoid coming out as rude. If only people would stop for a moment to acknowledge that not everyone feels the same way they do and that differences are OK, financial disputes may be avoided.

3. When requesting credit for an idea: It is usually to your advantage to collaborate with others when coming up with a plan or new idea. You'll gain more popularity if you're prepared to operate as a team.

However, there are times when it is preferable to prove that you alone deserve the credit. Use "I" while discussing your thoughts, for instance, if your manager emphasises self-sufficiency and you are vying for a promotion at work.

Cut down on "I" talk, and use "we" talk instead

The word "we" instantly evokes a sense of antiquity. We talk with an emphasis on similarities and shared experiences, which creates a sense of intimacy. You can do this in a subtle manner so that no one will notice. You don't need to modify the meaning of what you say. Just a few little adjustments will do.

Look at the examples below to see how this works: "I think the meeting starts at three."

"We have to be at the meeting room by three, right?" "I remember the summer of 2012. It was really hot." "We had a really hot summer in 2012."

"I think that house will be too expensive."

"We need to find out whether that house will be too expensive."

Put It Into Practice

Exercise I

You are going to keep track of how many "I"s you use today. Don't worry if you begin to lag behind. It's not necessary to completely remove the word "I." Just challenge yourself to stay aware of what you are saying.

Exercise II

Watch a conversation and count how many times each person starts a sentence with "I." Keep two running tests for a few minutes, one for each individual. Are the numbers close to being even? Do they both seem content with the way the conversation is going?

This exercise is particularly effective if you can observe two strangers since you won't know anything about their personal characteristics or the events they are debating. Every time I've tried it, I've noticed that if someone uses a lot of "I" talk, their conversation will start to seem monotonous. Keep this in mind the next time you catch yourself repeating "I" too frequently.

Day 7: Offer A Helping Hand

Giving and receiving assistance is a part of being human. Giving someone a helping hand when they require practical or emotional support is rewarding and can strengthen your relationship. Unfortunately, offering assistance isn't always easy. You will learn how to reach out to someone who is in need today.

Why asking someone if they need help can get complicated

There is a fine line between offering assistance to someone and making remarks that imply they are unqualified. If you don't approach the problem sensibly, the other party can feel oppressed. They can also think you're trying to meddle with their lives. On the other hand, refusing assistance can make you seem aloof and cold.

Here are some suggestions to help you strike the appropriate balance:

1. Explain to the person you are seeking assistance from why you are doing so in detail. When you do this, the other person will recognise that your offer is driven by a desire to make their life easier. Make it abundantly clear that you don't want to order them about.

Let's say, for example, that your friend has moved into a home that requires extensive maintenance. structural and economic work When you go to see them in their new house, you notice that it's a complete mess. Your acquaintance appears to be worn out and on the verge of tears.

They inform you that the house is proving to be a far larger project than they had anticipated. You want to offer to help your friend, but you don't want to treat them like a dunce by insinuating that they can't possibly complete the task on their own.

Which of the following questions do you believe would be most appropriate in this situation?

"Do you need help with this place?"

OR

"Hey, I've noticed that you seem really tired lately, and this house is a pretty big project. I'd love to help you. Could I come over this weekend and lend a hand with the wiring?"

The latter is more heartfelt since it demonstrates to your friend that you have taken the time to comprehend the difficulty they are experiencing. It implies that you have considered their situation and are not just making a vague offer of assistance because you believe they are unable to complete the task themselves.

2. Ask "How can I help?" or "Can I help by doing X?" instead of making a vague offer of assistance: Does the following situation sound familiar? You've had some bad news. You tell someone else about it. They say, "Just call me if you need help", or "If I can do anything, let me know".

These offers are well-intentioned, yet they are vague. They also sound stilted and formulaic. It's difficult to determine whether they were created just for political purposes.

What is the lesson here? Make your offer of assistance specific if you're doing so. If not, at least ask a question that offers the other person a chance to tell you what they need. Consider the daily challenges that someone in your situation could encounter.

For instance, you could discover that shopping for groceries and maintaining a clean home may seem burdensome if your friend's child is in the hospital. You could ask, "Can I help by doing a grocery run?" or "Would you like me to come over and do the housework for you?".

The same principles apply in the case of minor problems. If your colleague appears overworked and stressed one morning, don't just stand there and say, "You look busy, so let me know if you need help." It would be better to say, for example, "Can I help by doing that filing for you?" or "Would you like me to take the notes for this afternoon's meeting?"

3. Pay attention to helping someone change their circumstances rather than their character. Sometimes a person's problems are brought on by character flaws. For instance, if your friend lost their job because they are frequently late and have a tendency to daydream when sitting at their desk, they are to blame for their own issues because they failed to adhere to the fundamental standards of conduct expected of employees.

Your role in this situation is not to "fix" their character or to give them advice on how to live their lives, though. Yes, genuine personal transformation is possible, but it must originate from the individual and may call for professional assistance.

If they desire to change careers, you may help them look for a new job or conduct research on training providers. Telling someone about their own shortcomings and then expecting immediate change is pointless.

They probably already know what they need to work on and won't be interested in your imitative psychological analyses. In actuality, they will likely reject your attempts to intercede, which could harm your relationship. Offer helpful advice or offer to listen, but never attempt to "help" by changing someone's personality.

4. Don't offer emotional help or support unless you know you can remain nonjudgmental: Offering to help someone by "talking over a problem" or "just listening" is great – if you have the right skills.

Be sincere with yourself. Can you trust yourself to remain calm and listen if a friend or family member is going through a difficult time, even if they decide to do something you don't agree with? (This is especially crucial if their next actions could directly affect your own life.)

Help them find someone else who will be able to listen if you are unable to do so. Ideally, this person won't be emotionally invested in the situation.

5. If you want to contribute money, be flexible: If you have a friend or relative who is experiencing financial difficulties, you might want to assist them. Of course, assuming that you can afford it. However, many people are reluctant to accept money from friends and family because they are sensitive to the subject of money. Don't be shocked if someone declines your offer of financial assistance.

If someone is too proud to accept a present of money or if it violates their principles, you can either offer them a loan in its place (with no interest) or opportunities and services that will help them get back on their feet. For example, you may volunteer to babysit their children for free while they attend job interviews or connect them with professionals in your field.

Put It Into Practice

Do you know somebody who has been struggling lately? Call them and offer your assistance. Make sure you are aware of what you are capable of providing in advance and that you don't promise more than you can deliver.

Day 8: Practice Saying "Thank You"

One of the most important words in our language is "thank you." Human relationships are based not just on mutual acts of service but also on common interests and good communication. For instance, close friendships are built on the unspoken understanding that each friend will turn to the other when necessary.

Today, you will reflect on how frequently you express gratitude to others who offer assistance. Even self-made men and women require a helping hand or two to succeed.

Nobody appreciates ungrateful, whiny individuals who refuse to accept their good fortune. There are few things more annoying than someone who has numerous reasons to be grateful but constantly complains. Even less well-liked are those who get assistance from others but rarely bother to acknowledge it.

It doesn't matter how much prestige you have or how well-known you are; you are never "too good" to stop and express gratitude to everyone who helps you out. It's a simple way to establish a reputation as a cheerful, upbeat person who everyone likes to be around.

1. Construct a bridge Thank you for: A simple "Thank you" is always appreciated, but there is one trick that will make sure you leave a lasting impression. Tell someone specifically what has filled you with gratitude with a few additional words.

Imagine, for instance, that a coworker has agreed to attend a meeting on your behalf and take notes since you are urgently needed on a project. The majority of people would accept the notes and say, "Thank you so much!"

That's fine, but what do you think would happen if you used one of the following sentences in its place?

"Thank you for taking the time to make those notes for me." "Thank you for standing in for me and getting that information."

"Thank you for taking such detailed notes, that was so helpful of you."

These alternatives are special and personal. This tactic will let the other person feel valued for the work they have done, which will improve your relationship. It also keeps you from taking other people for granted.

For instance, if your partner serves dinner at most gatherings, you can notice that with time you stop expressing a noticable level of appreciation. Making an effort to demonstrate your appreciation for them will strengthen your relationship.

2. Offer to repay their kindness: If someone has gone above and beyond to help you, offering them assistance in return will show that you appreciate them. Most people won't agree to it, but they'll still be grateful that you asked. Ask, "How can I return the favor?" or "Is there anything I can do in return?"

You could also advise them to contact you for assistance if they have any future needs. Recall that relationships are based on giving and receiving. Both parties are willing to provide and receive assistance in a healthy friendship.

3. Never reject a complaint: I believe that the majority of you occasionally commit the crime of breaking a component or piece of property. Even a well-timed remark might make some of us blush with modesty, but arguing with someone who is trying to complement you is rude.

The only suitable response is a simple "Thank you," "I'm very glad you think so," or anything similar.

What if you believe that someone is only trying to insult you or is using sarcasm in their statement? You should still say "Thank you" because you will win regardless of what. If they are truly complimenting you, you win.

You still win if they are being arrogant or manipulative and you respond with "Thank you" before changing the subject since you haven't let them drag you down to their level.

Gratitude and mental health

Additionally, saying "Thank you" will help you feel grateful for what you have, which will make you happier. Research demonstrates that "gratitude journaling," or literally writing down what you are grateful for, improves mood and well-being. Even for those who have a chronic health problem, this is true.

When you start appreciating the good things in your life, you will naturally start to thank other people. It aids in the growth of a mindset that pushes you to identify possibilities rather than obstacles. Surprisingly, research has also revealed that those who receive appreciation for their efforts experience better mental health than those who feel underappreciated.

Put It into Practice

Exercise I

Your challenge today is to look for opportunities to express gratitude and thanks. There will undoubtedly be at least a few people that thank you. Let everyone know how much your gratitude for their assistance.

If someone simply holds the door open, look them in the eye and say, "Thanks a lot!" If you are unlucky enough to be the recipient of a significant act of kindness, let the other person know how much you value them.

Exercise II

Take it a step further, if you can, and take the time to express to a loved one how much you appreciate their continued assistance and support. You may even call them up and tell them how amazing they are!

One day, I realised I had never expressed my gratitude to my mother for all of the support she had provided me during my time in college, particularly during the times I struggled to stay focused.

That evening, I called to let her know how important her love and support had been for me as I pursued my academic goals. Although I should have made that call years ago, I informed her that I believed it was better to make it now than never. She was taken aback before bursting into joyful tears.

Never underestimate the impact of a simple "Thank you."

Day 9: Stop Trying To Score Points

I will admit that I enjoy being correct, and I am not the only person who feels this way. We all have our own points of view, and it's satisfying when we know—or at least believe we know—best.

The difficulty arises when we attempt to validate our opinions just for the sake of winning points or convincing someone else that they were mistaken the entire time.

If you've ever spent hours trying to convince someone to accept your point of view on a problem or situation, don't be too hard on yourself. We all completed it. I didn't give up on the idea of "winning" every argument until I was in my mid-20s.

When I was younger, I believed that I had somehow failed or exposed myself as weak unless I forced my weak opponent to admit that I was "right." I didn't really care that much about the subject of the conversation half the time. My main concern was demonstrating how much better I was than everyone else in the room.

Looking back, I'm ashamed of my younger self. He was so busy trying to persuade everyone of his so-called intelligence that he missed the opportunity to establish some nice friendships and sexual relationships.

I used to wonder why my dates hardly ever developed into something deeper. It seems so obvious right away! Not many women will put up with self-righteous men who enjoy explaining why their viewpoints are completely incorrect.

Needless to say, a confrontational approach doesn't provide the foundation for a healthy friendship or romantic relationship and it can also drive your relationships insane. Every now and again having a dispute is entertaining, but frequently arguing is tiresome.

You're familiar with the proverb, "Sometimes, being happy is more important than being right"? That is what I am referring to here. Let rid of the inconsequential minor debates and reserve your thinking skills for what matters.

Let me explain what I mean in this chapter. I'm not referring about those situations where you actually need to alter someone's mindset. For instance, if your husband wants to relocate to a city where you believe it would be better for both of you to stay in the country, you would need to file a case against the move. That makes common sense.

It is wrong to impose your views on someone in order to win an argument if you want them to like you and open up to you. By all means, exchange ideas and opinions, but be mindful of the moment when you switch from a constructive dialogue to a pettiness debate.

Why point scoring is, well, pointless

Keep in mind that scoring points rarely succeeds in any way. The more aggressively you push someone and the more convinced you are that you are right and they are wrong, the more probable it is that they will begin to shut down. There is a strong neurologic explanation for this phenomenon.

When we find ourselves in a potentially dangerous scenario, our fight-or-flight reaction kicks in with high vigour. The parts of the brain responsible for logic and reasoning experience a decline in activity, and the parts of the brain connected to conflict are triggered to act.

The outcome? We become less and less interested in actually assessing the evidence that someone else presents and instead focus on fighting back. This is why two people can be having a reasoned conversation one minute and then yelling and screaming at each other the next.

In the long run, you might suffer even if you "win" a debate. You can never be sure if someone gives in because you were able to persuade them of your viewpoint or if they simply stopped engaging with you because they were tired of the whole affair.

Conflict might result in eviction if certain issues are not addressed. Just though you appear to have succeeded in bulldozing your opponent doesn't mean they will forget about it any time soon. If you want to keep your relationship intact, make sure that any significant underlying issues have actually been resolved.

Pay attention to your emotional state. It's a safe bet that whatever comes out of your mouth won't be helpful or constructive if you're feeling tense, angry, or like you want to punch a wall.

Another telltale sign that you're more interested in arguing points than having a fruitful discussion is a sudden discovery that you can't even recall what triggered the argument in the first place and you don't really care!

If you're still not convinced, consider how much more at ease you'll feel if you give up the notion that you must always have the last word. Wouldn't it be good to know that you are under no obligation to start analysing anything someone says if their point of view differs from your own?

If you enjoy the tension of a heated debate, why not participate in a philosophical discussion? group or societal debate? Choose a more logical outlet for your dramatic tendency. Don't let it destroy your relationship.

Put It Into Practice

You're going to let other folks to be mistaken today. This will be difficult if you have to spend time with someone whose worldview differs from your own, but that is the whole point.

You won't waste your time or breath trying to convince them that their opinion is false and worthless. Where has it gotten you before? Nowhere, most likely. What impact does point scoring have on your relationships? Nothing!

If you need to leave a situation in order to avoid an argument, that is OK, but try to work things out. This activity will demonstrate to you that the world does not end when other individuals perceive things in a different way.

You'll soon discover that there is enough room in the world for opinions of all kinds. Nobody has a moral obligation to agree with you. You are not required to persuade people of your viewpoints either.

Day 10: Ask Questions That Get Results

What do you do when you need to discover information quickly? Of course, ask questions! It ought to be so easy, right? Unfortunately, as you are aware, getting clear answers from other people is not always simple.

You can't make somebody give you an answer, but you may greatly improve your chances of getting one by refining the questions you ask.

Here is how to obtain answers:

1. Build up naturally to queries under pressure. Nobody enjoys having a significant question thrust upon them. Demonstrate some empathy for their position. For instance, let's imagine you want to ask your manager some questions about your chances of getting a raise the following year.

Ask them if it's a good time to talk about your position at the company and your expectations for the future rather than changing the subject right away and asking if you believe your salary will get a boost.

2. Decide if an open or closed question is preferable. We were frequently instructed that asking open questions—those that begin with "Why" and "How"—is a better

strategy than asking closed inquiries that can only be resolved with a "YES" or "NO."

Although the form will produce more detailed responses, this isn't always a good thing. For instance, if you're speaking to someone who has a reputation for rambling on without getting to the point, it could be best to use a closed question instead.

3. Use a four-part structure when assisting someone with a problem. Questions help you with more than just getting information. They are a great way to support someone during a difficult time.

Empathy and sympathy will only go you so far. Asking the right questions will enable someone to develop a strategy that addresses the core of the issue.

Irène Leonard, an executive coach, suggests using a four-step approach:

A. Ask someone questions that will help them hone in on their issue.

“What seems to be the issue here?” is a good starting point.

B. Obtain further information. Once you have established the underlying cause of their distress, you can then use prompts to get the full story, if necessary. Questions like

"Can you tell me more about that?" and "What else can you tell me?" are useful in this context.

C. Ask them questions that will help them achieve their ideal outcome. Ask them specifically to describe what a successful solution would entail for you. Find out what they want to happen, what their priorities are, and how they prefer to solve the problem. Do they want to figure things out on their own, with a friend, or with the help of a third party, for example?

D. Ask them questions that will aid them in determining their next steps. For example, you could ask them whether they have any firm ideas about how they plan to proceed and how they will know when they have achieved their goals.

4. Don't lead people to a specific response. Asking a question in an objective manner will help you learn what someone truly thinks about an idea. In other words, you should refrain from posing leading questions. Consider how you phrase them.

Here are three examples of tricky questions that nudge a respondent to provide a particular kind of response:

"Does everyone agree that we should streamline the department?"

"Don't you think that we should spend Thanksgiving at Peter's house this year?"

“Shouldn’t we put this into action as soon as possible?”

If you asked these questions, you would be creating your own foundational plan. If someone objected vehemently, they might do so, but most people like an easy life. Open questions frequently encourage poor decision-making at both home and business, which can be disastrous.

This is even more likely if you have a strong personality because few individuals will be willing to challenge your assumptions and way of thinking.

Let’s look at a better way to ask those questions:

“What does everyone think we should do with regards to the department’s structure?”

“Where do you think we should spend Thanksgiving this year?” “When do you think we should put this plan into action?”

5. Don't make people choose between two or three options. This strategy implies that you have already considered all of your options. There may be viable options, but if you ask questions in this format, you will never know.

It's more effective to just ask someone for their suggestions or to state the obvious, such as, "How would you handle this situation?"

6. Be ready for the unexpected. Never presume to know what someone else is going to say in advance. Give them your undivided attention and be prepared with a few phrases you can use if they share any startling information.

"Thank you for telling me – I need time to process that," "This is a surprise, can I have a minute to take that on board?" and "I'll admit this has shocked me a little, but I'd like to talk about it further," can all help smooth over an awkward situation.

Even more advice on the art of asking questions may be found in my book, The Science of Effective Communication: Improve Your Small Talk and Social Skills, Develop Chrarama, and Learn How to Talk to Anyone.

Put It Into Practice

You will use the aforementioned guidelines today when asking questions. Now is the ideal time if you've been meaning to get clarity on a matter for a while but haven't gotten around to it! These inquiries don't need to be particularly important.

The goal is to practise receiving the information you need while still having a positive interaction. Put your listening skills to good use whenever the other person responds with an answer, don't forget.

CONCLUSION

Steps to Effective Communication

The two most important words: Thank You

The three most important words: All is forgiven

The four most important words: What is your opinion

The Five most important words: You did a good job

The six most important words: I want to understand you better

The least important word: "I"

The Power of Listening: Nothing will sabotage efficient communication more quickly than one party not paying attention to the other. This recently occurred to a client of the University of Michigan's financial assistance office, where his child attends school. Since his child first attended that office in 2009, every single person he has dealt with there has been brief, abrupt, and robotic when explaining the Federal requirements for student aid. The fact that they stick to a budget and don't think outside the box completely disorients him as the recipient of financial aid when he attended Western Michigan University years ago. His assumption was that the financial aid office exists to help students find a way to pay for their education when they don't have enough money to cover the total cost.

Employees at the University of Michigan's financial aid office make it clear through their words and nonverbal communication that their goal is to reduce the amount of funds allocated to each student in order to achieve a secret budget goal. He tried explaining this to the department head on several occasions, and each time, she circulated it and blamed him for misunderstood the counsellors, failing to follow their guidelines, or taking what was said out of context. She never acknowledged that she had heard what my client was saying or that she would work to get him financial aid to cover the $26,000 annual expense of attending school. His child asked, "How can I find more money to go to school?" The counselor responded, "By getting married, having a baby, joining the military or your parents dying." He said, "None of those are a remote possibility, to which he responded, "Well maybe you should have chosen a school that was more affordable to you." His child worked hard to get accepted to U of M and he worked hard to save enough money for him to go there.

Actually, the counsellor was explaining to him the federal regulations governing student aid, but the manner in which he did so was completely inappropriate. My client was quite defensive and blamed the entire problem on me when she brought it to the department director's attention since he refused to accept that these were the guidelines. That wasn't the idea, but rather there are proper and improper ways to say "no," which is exactly what they were telling his son to do in order to become more agitated. In their last conversation, my client's department head said, "Please accept my apologies for any response you feel was inappropriate." Despite the fact that my client felt the comments were inappropriate, they were. He totally Understands the Federal Guidelines, and she frequently and sarcastically recounted them to him, driving home the point. Putting the blame back on my client and his son made it clear that neither of them ever paid attention to what I was trying to convey and that my client was not heard. That unfortunate gap between a parent and a key function at a significant institution is regrettable.

Controlling Conflict: Saying that my client had a conflict with the University of Michigan financial aid office is an understatement. It was a significant breakdown in communication, one for which I'm confident he will pay the price in the future — literally. However, having disagreement at home, at business, or in any other setting where two or more people are exchanging information is a regular part of life. What matters is how we handle conflict and bring it to a successful conclusion. My client has agreed to agree, accept what the financial aid office will give, and find another source of funding to make up the difference in tuition in the case of the financial aid office. He can live with the fact that the head of that office will never understand what was said to her; it is her loss. There are several successful strategies for getting out of a sticky situation, but one of them is to decide what you can live with and what you won't budge on. Knowing that conflict occurs and having the tools necessary to navigate it and resolve it are essential for maintaining the proper frame of mind as it takes place.

My client's situation was unfortunate but not personal, and I guarantee that he is neither the first nor the last to encounter a brick wall when dealing with the University of Michigan financial assistance office. This was brought to a logical end with the help of removing the emotion and defusing the situation.

How Your Attitude Affects Communication: Every attitude is a combination of feelings, beliefs, and assessments. Behavior refers to the actions or reactions of an object or organisation, and attitude influences behaviour. Persuasive communication modifies attitudes, which in turn alters behaviour, which in turn creates a more productive environment. Persuasive communication entails openly attempting to persuade someone else to change their behaviour, and it only functions when the source is reliable and trustworthy. Establishing trust and credibility initially with your coworkers and other important relationships you have provides a solid foundation. The keys of persuasion include learning how to state your case properly, support it with arguments, and win others on to your point of view.

Giving and Receiving Feedback: We can give or receive feedback as a kind of communication. Sometimes, feedback is referred to as "critic," however this severely limits its significance.

People can learn from feedback how effective they are at what they're trying to accomplish or how they affect you. It gives us a way to understand how our actions affect the world around us and makes us more effective. Knowing how other people perceive us will help us solve communication and interaction issues. Of course, there are two sides to it: giving and receiving feedback.

Getting Feedback: Some people view input as pure criticism and do not want to hear it. Others view it as a confirmation of their worthlessness and as spiritually crushing. Others still only want to hear praise, but nothing that would imply effect. Of course, it isn't the case for everyone. Some people are willing to accept feedback and seek it out even if it is occasionally upsetting because they believe they can grow from it. It all depends on whether you think feedback will help you or hurt you.

This is not to imply that we always have to accept feedback or the manner in which it is occasionally provided. We all have the option to decline food, and we may anticipate receiving it in a respectful and supportive manner. But there is an opposite to every great and open way of receiving criticism—a negative and closed way that pushes feedback away and keeps it at bay.

Negative/Closed Style

Defense: defends individual actions, frequently objects to money returned. Attacking: verbally criticises the feedback provider and flips the script. Denies the accuracy or falsity of the crowdsourcing. Disrespectful: diminishes the speaker, what the speaker is saying, or the speaker's right to respond. Closed: Ignores the criticism and listens flatly without interest. Ineffective listening: makes no effort to "hear" or comprehend the feedback's meaning. Finding explanations for the feedback that remove any personal responsibility is rationalisation. patronising: yes, but with such little interest. Superb: listens and agrees, but expresses the opinion that the feedback will not have much of an actual impact.

Positive/Open Style

Open: listens without interruptions or objections frequently. A responsive person is open to hearing what is being said without turning the table. Accepting: Take the criticism without rebuke. Respectful: acknowledges the importance of what is being said and the speaker's right to say it. Engaged: appropriately engages the speaker, seeking clarification as necessary. Active listening is paying close attention and attempting to understand what is being said. Thoughtful: aims to comprehend the personal behaviour that has caused the feedback. Interested: I'm genuinely interested in hearing feedback. Sincere desire to make personal changes, if appropriate.

Giving Feedback

The opposite of feedback is providing it. Some people deliver feedback in a harsh manner; after all, it's simpler to give counsel than to accept it. Some people use feedback as a weapon or provide it as payback. Feedback is a terrific method to be critical of others. Because feedback might be received in a very negative way, how you deliver it is just as important as how you accept it.

You must be attentive, sensitive, and honest when providing feedback if you want to be effective. There are effective and ineffective ways to give feedback, just as there are positive and negative approaches to absorbing it.

Ineffective/Negative Delivery

Attacking involves hard hitting and aggressing while focusing on the other person's vulnerabilities. Indirect: feedback that is ambiguous and issues that are hinted at rather than immediately addressed. Little consideration for the needs of the other person. Respectful: The feedback is changing, bordering on injuring. Feedback that is judgmental judges a person's character rather than their actions. General: aimed at broad issues that are difficult to describe. Poor timing: given long after the prompting event or at the last minute. Impulsive: given carelessly or with little regard for the consequences. Selfish: Feedback meets the requirements of the giver rather than those of the recipient.

Effective/Positive Delivery

Supportive: given in a way that is non-threatening and uplifting. The focus of the feedback is clearly stated. Sensitive: delivered with consideration for the needs of the other person. Respectful: Feedback is not intended to offend or degrade. Descriptive: concentrates on variable behaviour rather than personality. Specific: feedback is targeted at certain behaviours or events. Healthy timing: delivered as soon after the triggering event as possible and at a convenient time. Thoughtful: better regarded than impulsive. Helpful: comments are meant to be valuable to the other person.

The Importance of Feedback

For people who want to establish genuine interactions, feedback is a must. Giving feedback connects us and our behaviour to the environment around us, making it a powerful and significant communication tool.

Communication in the Digital Age: There are now several ways to hinder communication between people, such texting, Facebooking, Twittering, instant messaging, voice mail, and email, to mention a few. The Time Management Program by Stephen Covey exhorts us to master technology rather than allowing it to be our master. I recently attended a baseball game, and as I looked across the stadium, I noticed a sea of people staring at their cell phones. They were texting, taking pictures, uploading them to Facebook, and conversing; this was a new era of mass media. I frequently receive urgent messages from clients and potential clients asking me detailed questions about life-changing events and expecting a straightforward response in return. In the digital age, it can be challenging to communicate effectively unless we learn how to use these tools persuasively and appropriately. An employee of Mine has a client who routinely throws off chasing emails.

My client consistently complains about the employee who is seen as being conflictual and aggressive. I suggested that she sit down with the employee, show her examples of the inappropriate emails, suggest a 24-hour "cool down" period, and then initially discuss the emails with someone they can trust before pressing the send button. A month later, the client reported that nine out of ten emails were discarded before being sent. The employee then learned the art of refraining from responding by email to additional communications that were upsetting her. In current economic context, where we are doing much more with much less and tensions are high, it is especially crucial.

Ask yourself the following inquiries:

How would your personal and professional lives change if you were able to master these fundamental skills? Can you afford to put off making the investment to enhance your communication? You'll be shocked at the dramatic swing your life will take after you learn how to communicate effectively. Did you know that the most valuable asset to a company or a client is a person who communicates well, someone with the capacity to influence and persuade others? Are you speaking effectively and successfully to influence others, or are you just talking?

Last but not least, Improve Your Communication Skills by Using These Communicative Techniques:

Developing stronger communication abilities can be gratifying and meaningful. You may advance in your job and create lasting social connections by improving your communication abilities.

There are numerous ways to improve communication in our natural world. But developing our intrapersonal communication abilities is the first step. Everybody has that inner voice that constantly speaks to them in both positive and negative ways. The way we react to such statements, though, reveals how we speak to ourselves. The posture of a person might reveal whether or not they have effective intrapersonal communication skills.

To communicate effectively, one must have self-worth. Have you ever had a conversation with a low self-esteem person? A person with low self-esteem will typically mumble, talk with their head down, make little eye contact, have poor posture, and use incorrect body language. Such individuals could find it challenging to attain leadership positions (e.g., manager, supervisor, or boss) and establish dominance over others.

Many people are unsure of where to start when trying to improve their speaking abilities. The easiest place to start is with the "parts of speech mechanism." I am unable to be exhaustive or cover all the aspects of speech in this short post. However, if you are serious about enhancing your speech—and I assume you are since you are reading this—you can look out a speech language pathologist (speech therapist) to assist you in enhancing the areas that require improvement.

The following tactics could help you develop your oral (speaking) abilities. I'm not going to give you these tips in any specific order. Some methods may be more crucial than others depending on where you are in your life at that particular moment.

Pragmatics:

1) Placement. Your prospects in the workplace rise when you establish yourself as an useful individual through your expressive (oral, speaking) communicative abilities. The art of speaking and writing is grammar. Your ability to effectively use semantic and syntactic structures may improve as you gain more control over these talents.

Knowing the meaning of words and utilising them correctly are both semantic. A complex sentence, which consists of two or more simple sentences connected by one or more connective words, or a simple sentence with a subjective verb agreement, are examples of sentences that are grammatically organised in a clear and exact form by the use of syntax.

You can rise up the success ladder and improve your credibility by knowing how to employ complex words with imbedded indirect meanings correctly. People tend to believe those who utilise the English language so well.

When you correctly apply grammar rules, you come out as more credible.

2) Receptive speech. Your ability to engage with others can be improved by being receptive to your surroundings. Understanding your environment and responding appropriately to its components is referred to as receptive language. Without a solid awareness of your ability to interpret others' language, you run the risk of misreading them rather frequently. The skeleton, or core, as some could put it, of communicative techniques is the components of speech. The mechanism for parts of speech is as follows: adjective, pronoun, verb, adverb, preposition, conjunction, interjection, and noun.

3. Consciousness Your ability to deliver presentations orally can be improved by becoming more aware of how you pronounce your words. You can attain extraordinary success by working on your diction to appropriately produce sounds and phonemes in words, phrases, and

sentences. When you speak with poise, people will become emotionally invested in your dialogues or presentation skills.

One of language's fundamental building blocks is articulation. The capacity to accurately form sounds (phonemes) in words is known as articulation. Sounds each have unique personalities.

Our articulatory structures and voices help us to form speech. Instead of the lungs, the throat, palate, teeth, tongue, lips, and nostrils are responsible for articulation.

The vowel sound or sounds are a straightforward, articulate sound made by a consistent effusion of breath and a particular shape of the mouth.

Different types of consonants, such as those made by the lips, teeth, palate, and nose, are separated.

The pronunciation of words with accent, quantity, emphasis, pause, and tone is known as prosody.

Accent is the placing of a unique voice stress on a certain letter or syllable of a word so that it may be better heard than the others or distinguishable from them. For example, in the word suppose, the accent must be placed on the letter u and the second syllable, "sume."

Ideas leave their marks in words. Any ambiguity in the marks could make the concepts they stand for unclear.

Setting objectives. Setting goals is crucial if you want to improve your speaking abilities. Setting goals entails developing both long-term and short-term objectives as well as an action plan. When your objectives are on paper, they are simpler to follow. It's acceptable to modify or revise your goals as you go. Your initial objectives might not always be realistic. Your short-term objectives should help you achieve your long-term objectives.

Modulation (5). The ability to modulate your voice allows you to use it in expressive ways. Your speaking abilities may come alive if you can find the vocal tones that come naturally to you. In the comfort of your own home and in public places, practise different tones. The tone you are employing is not your natural voice if it gets scratchy or worn out. The modulation procedure should have appropriate breath assistance from your diaphragm.

6) Mentality. A positive outlook and tenacity are essential for developing improved communication abilities.

7) Resilience. Being in perpetual training mode is tenacity. No great speaker has ever achieved success without diligent and steadfast preparation. Great speakers are able to overcome obstacles by honing their voices through practise. They pick up how to set up and organise things. They improved their capacity for imparting knowledge to others.

8) Creativity. Imagine what it will be like once you have learned the techniques for speaking in front of anyone effectively. Practice the techniques in the comfort of your own home in front of a mirror as you imagine (visualise), then progressively apply them in your surroundings. Self-improvement is essential for improving your public speaking abilities. You will gain more self-assurance in your speaking abilities as you apply these techniques in your environment.

9) Enthusiasm. Eloquence in speech is a hallmark of charismatic leadership. Your vocal expression and verbal expression—your voice and speech—should be loaded with a variety of vibrant tones to compel people to act, and your word choice should be compelling and uttered with excitement. Your genuineness, illumination, and humanity in your storytelling move others. Excellent speakers are created, not born. Without rigorous and persistent practise, no great communicator has ever reached their top performance.

Leaders with charisma understand the three components of a good storey. The backdrop or circumstance in which the storey is composed, the mood that the characters create, and the plot or the activity that the characters engage in make up the three elements. Find out what your audience wants and needs, then give them a way to get it.

CPSIA information can be obtained
at www.ICGtesting.com
Printed in the USA
LVHW012111291122
734192LV00014B/658

9 781944 237257